KID CHEMISTRY LAB

INVESTIGATING ATOMS & MOLECULES

Jessica Rusick

Checkerboard Library

An Imprint of Abdo Publishing
abdobooks.com

ABDOBOOKS.COM

Published by Abdo Publishing, a division of ABDO, PO Box 398166, Minneapolis, Minnesota 55439.

Printed in the United States of America, North Mankato, Minnesota
052022
092022

Design and Production: Kelly Doudna, Mighty Media, Inc.
Editor: Liz Salzmann
Cover Photograph: FatCamera/iStockphoto
Interior Photographs: AJ_Watt/iStockphoto, p. 21; carlofranco/iStockphoto, p. 17; Designua/Shutterstock Images, p. 19; julie deshaies/Shutterstock Images, pp. 8–9; Lia Gloss/Shutterstock Images, p. 23; Library of Congress/Wikimedia Commons, p. 11; Mighty Media, Inc., pp. 26, 27, 28, 29; momemoment/Shutterstock Images, p. 7; Monkey Business Images/Shutterstock Images, p. 5; Nasky/Shutterstock Images, pp. 13, 15; triloks/iStockphoto, p. 25

Library of Congress Control Number: 2021953161

Publisher's Cataloging-in-Publication Data
Names: Rusick, Jessica, author.
Title: Investigating atoms & molecules / by Jessica Rusick.
Description: Minneapolis, Minnesota : Abdo Publishing, 2023 | Series: Kid chemistry lab | Includes online resources and index.
Identifiers: ISBN 9781532199028 (lib. bdg.) | ISBN 9781098272951 (ebook)
Subjects: LCSH: Chemistry--Juvenile literature. | Atoms--Juvenile literature. | Molecules--Juvenile literature. | Science projects--Juvenile literature.
Classification: DDC 540--dc23

CONTENTS

Chapter 1

WHAT ARE ATOMS & MOLECULES?

Atoms are the building blocks of all matter. Matter is anything that takes up space. It includes all solids, liquids, and gases.

Matter is made of elements. Elements are substances that can't be broken down into simpler parts. Atoms are the smallest pieces of elements. Each element is made of one type of atom. Gold is an element. It is made entirely of gold atoms.

Atoms can form new substances by bonding together into molecules. Water is made of water molecules. A water molecule is two **hydrogen** atoms bonded with one oxygen atom. Atoms can combine into millions of different molecules.

Atoms are very tiny. There are trillions of atoms in each of your body's cells!

Chapter 2

ATOMS & MOLECULES BASICS

All of a substance's molecules are made of the same number and types of atoms. For example, every **hydrogen** peroxide molecule is made of two hydrogen atoms and two oxygen atoms. Molecules have different **properties** than the atoms that form them. Hydrogen and oxygen are both colorless gases. But hydrogen peroxide is a pale blue liquid.

Substances made of more than one element are called compounds. Hydrogen peroxide is a compound because it contains two elements, hydrogen and oxygen. Molecules can also contain only atoms of the same element. The oxygen we breathe is made only of oxygen molecules. These are two atoms of oxygen bonded together.

Hydrogen peroxide can be used to clean wounds and surfaces.

Molecules are written as molecular **formulas**. In a molecular formula, letters stand for different elements. Small numbers show how many atoms of each element are in the molecule. The molecular formula for **hydrogen** peroxide is H_2O_2. *H* stands for hydrogen and *O* stands for oxygen.

PERIODIC TABLE

- Nonmetal
- Alkali metal
- Alkaline earth metal
- Transition metal
- Metal
- Metalloid
- Halogen

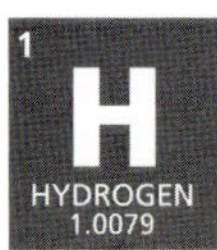 1 **H** HYDROGEN 1.0079								
 3 **Li** LITHIUM 6.941	4 **Be** BERYLLIUM 9.0122							
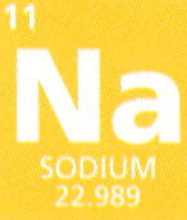 11 **Na** SODIUM 22.989	12 **Mg** MAGNESIUM 24.305							
19 **K** POTASSIUM 39.098	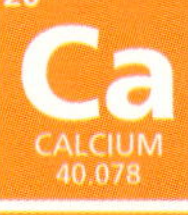 20 **Ca** CALCIUM 40.078	 21 **Sc** SCANDIUM 44.955	 22 **Ti** TITANIUM 47.867	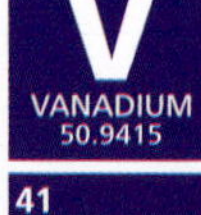 23 **V** VANADIUM 50.9415	 24 **Cr** CHROMIUM 51.9961	 25 **Mn** MANGANESE 54.938	 26 **Fe** IRON 55.845	 27 **Co** COBALT 58.933
37 **Rb** RUBIDIUM 85.467	 38 **Sr** STRONTIUM 87.62	 39 **Y** YTTRIUM 88.9058	40 **Zr** ZICRONIUM 91.224	41 **Nb** NIOBIUM 92.9063	42 **Mo** MOLYBDENUM 95.95	43 **Tc** TECHNETIUM (98)	44 **Ru** RUTHENIUM 101.07	45 **Rh** RHODIUM 102.90
55 **Cs** CAESIUM 132.905	56 **Ba** BARIUM 137.327	57-71*	 72 **Hf** HAFNIUM 178.49	 73 **Ta** TANTALUM 180.94	 74 **W** TUNGSTEN 183.84	 75 **Re** RHENIUM 186.207	 76 **Os** OSMIUM 190.23	 77 **Ir** IRIDIUM 192.217
87 **Fr** FRANCIUM (223)	 88 **Ra** RADIUM (226)	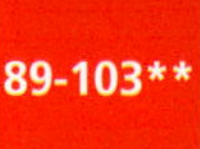 89-103**	 104 **Rf** RUTHERFORDIUM (267)	 105 **Db** DUBNIUM (268)	 106 **Sg** SEABORGIUM (271)	 107 **Bh** BOHRIUM (272)	 108 **Hs** HASSIUM (270)	 109 **Mt** MEITNERIUM (276)

*	 57 **La** LANTHANUM 138.90	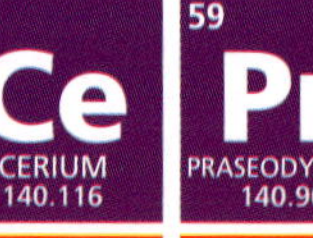 58 **Ce** CERIUM 140.116	59 **Pr** PRASEODYMIUM 140.90	 60 **Nd** NEODYMIUM 144.242	 61 **Pm** PROMETHIUM (145)	 62 **Sm** SAMARIUM 150.36	63 **Eu** EUROPIUM 151.964
**	 89 **Ac** ACTINIUM (227)	90 **Th** THORIUM 232.0377	 90 **Pa** PROTACTINIUM 231.03	 92 **U** URANIUM 238.02	93 **Np** NEPTUNIUM (237)	 94 **Pu** PLUTONIUM (244)	 95 **Am** AMERICIUM (243)

The periodic table of the elements contains basic information about all 118 known elements.

OF THE ELEMENTS

- Noble gas
- Actinide
- Lanthanide

  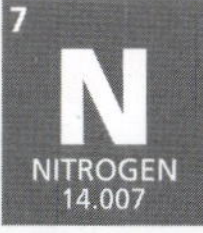 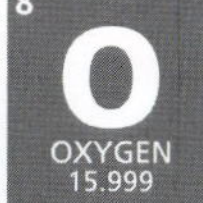 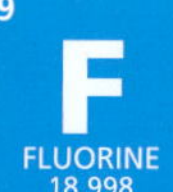       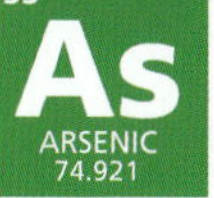         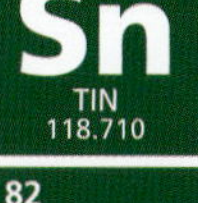 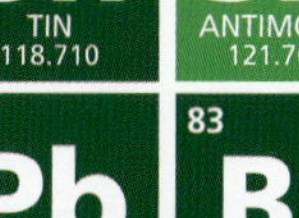  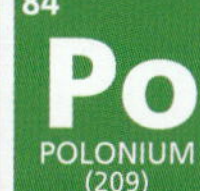          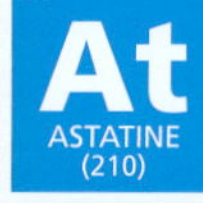           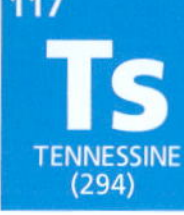 

								2 He HELIUM 4.0026
			5 B BORON 10.811	6 C CARBON 12.011	7 N NITROGEN 14.007	8 O OXYGEN 15.999	9 F FLUORINE 18.998	10 Ne NEON 20.1797
			13 Al ALUMINIUM 26.981	14 Si SILICON 28.085	15 P PHOSPHORUS 30.974	16 S SULFUR 32.066	17 Cl CHLORINE 35.453	18 Ar ARGON 39.948
28 Ni NICKEL 58.6934	29 Cu COPPER 63.546	30 Zn ZINC 65.38	31 Ga GALLIUM 69.723	32 Ge GERMANIUM 72.63	33 As ARSENIC 74.921	34 Se SELENIUM 78.971	35 Br BROMINE 79.904	36 Kr KRYPTON 83.798
46 Pd PALLADIUM 106.42	47 Ag SILVER 107.8682	48 Cd CADMIUM 112.414	49 In INDIUM 114.818	50 Sn TIN 118.710	51 Sb ANTIMONY 121.760	52 Te TELLURIUM 127.60	53 I IODINE 126.90	54 Xe XENON 131.293
78 Pt PLATINUM 195.084	79 Au GOLD 196.96	80 Hg MERCURY 200.59	81 Tl THALLIUM 204.38	82 Pb LEAD 207.2	83 Bi BISMUTH 208.98	84 Po POLONIUM (209)	85 At ASTATINE (210)	86 Rn RADON (222)
110 Ds DARMSTADTIUM (281)	111 Rg ROENTGENIUM (280)	112 Cn COPERNICIUM (285)	113 Uut UNUNTRIUM (284)	114 Fl FLEROVIUM (289)	115 Uup UNUNPENTIUM (288)	116 Lv LIVERMORIUM (293)	117 Ts TENNESSINE (294)	118 Og OGANESSON (294)

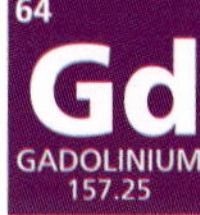   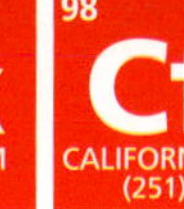  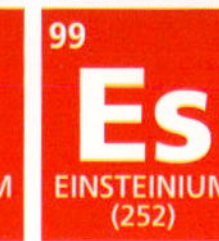 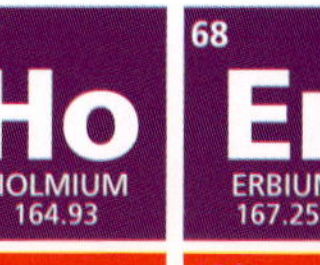       

64 Gd GADOLINIUM 157.25	65 Tb TERIBIUM 158.92	66 Dy DYSPROSIUM 162.500	67 Ho HOLMIUM 164.93	68 Er ERBIUM 167.259	69 Tm THULIUM 168.93	70 Yb YTTERBIUM 173.054	71 Lu LUTETIUM 174.9668
96 Cm CURIUM (247)	97 Bk BERKELIUM (247)	98 Cf CALIFORNIUM (251)	99 Es EINSTEINIUM (252)	100 Fm FERMIUM (257)	101 Md MENDELEVIUM (258)	102 No NOBELIUM (259)	103 Lr LAWRENCIUM (262)

Chapter 3

ATOMIC DISCOVERIES

Chemistry is the study of matter. Chemists study atoms and molecules to develop new medicines and other products. Chemists also work to develop safer and better ways to produce food, electricity, and more.

In 1808, British chemist John Dalton proposed a new atomic theory. It states that matter is made of atoms, and that each element is made of one type of atom. Dalton's theory also states that atoms combine in whole numbers to form compounds.

In the 1910s, British scientist Ernest Rutherford discovered more about atoms. Through experiments, Rutherford found that atoms are made of very small particles. These are called **protons**, **neutrons**, and electrons. Rutherford's discoveries helped scientists better understand how atoms function.

Ernest Rutherford

PROTONS, NEUTRONS & ELECTRONS

Atoms are made of protons, neutrons, and electrons. Protons and neutrons are in the center of an atom. This area is called the nucleus. The number of protons in an atom determines what element it is. An atom with one proton is a **hydrogen** atom. An atom with two protons is a **helium** atom. Hydrogen and helium are both elements.

Electrons travel around the atom's nucleus in circles. These circles are called shells. Most atoms have more than one shell. Each shell can hold a certain number of electrons. The inner shell can hold up to two electrons. Outer shells can hold up to eight electrons. Once a shell is full, electrons fill more outer shells. The more electrons an atom has, the more shells it has to hold them.

PARTS OF AN ATOM

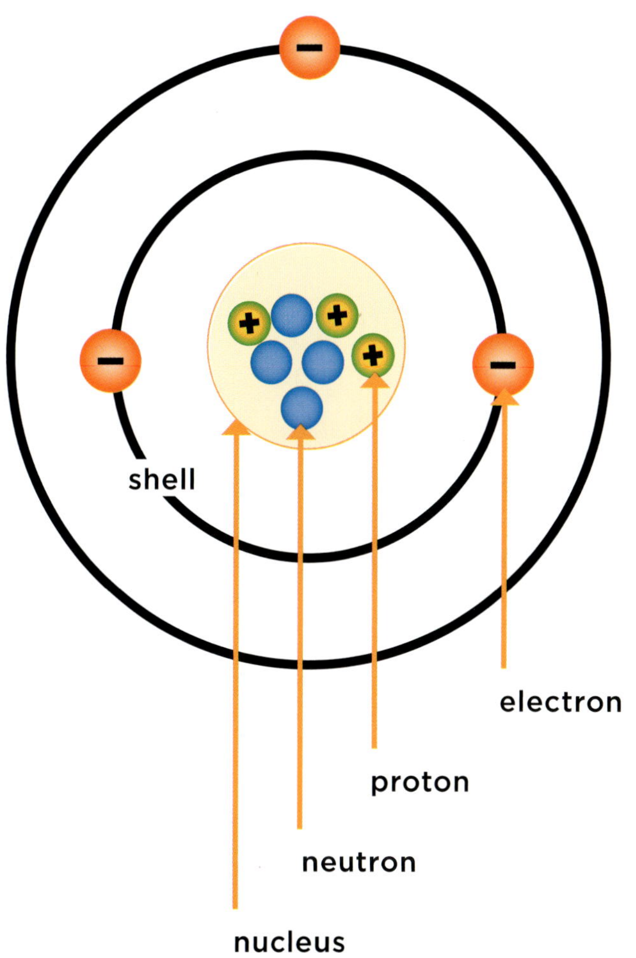

For example, **aluminum** atoms have 13 electrons. Two electrons fill the inner shell. Eight electrons fill the second shell. The remaining three electrons are in the third shell.

The last shell of an atom is called the valence shell. Electrons in the valence shell are called valence electrons. Valence electrons determine how atoms bond with each other to form molecules.

Scientists have discovered several types of chemical bonds. Two of the most common types are covalent bonds and ionic bonds. Valence electrons play a role in both of these types of bonds.

ATOMIC SHELLS

Helium atoms have one shell.

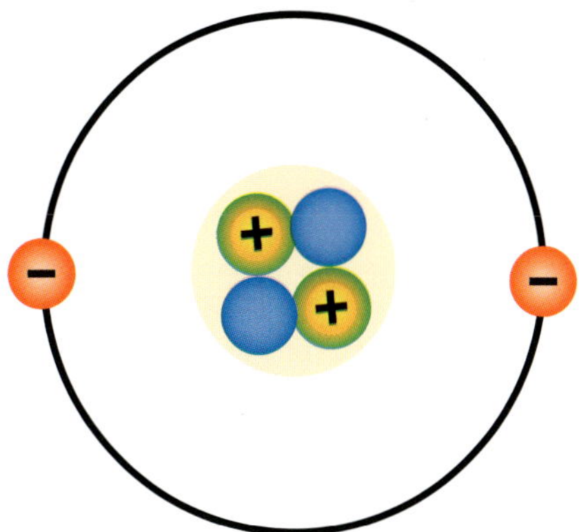

Lithium atoms have two shells.

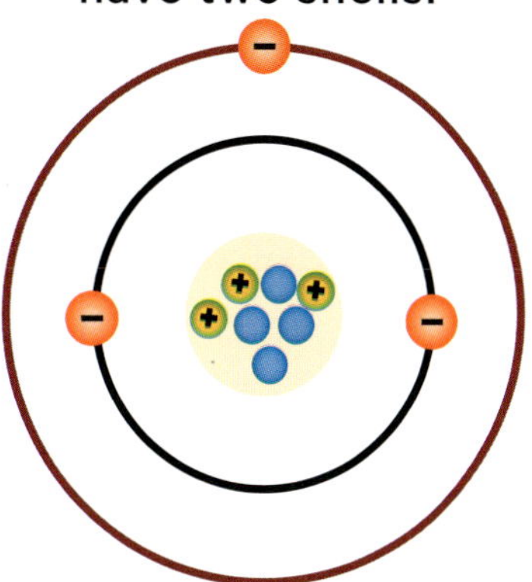

Aluminum atoms have three shells.

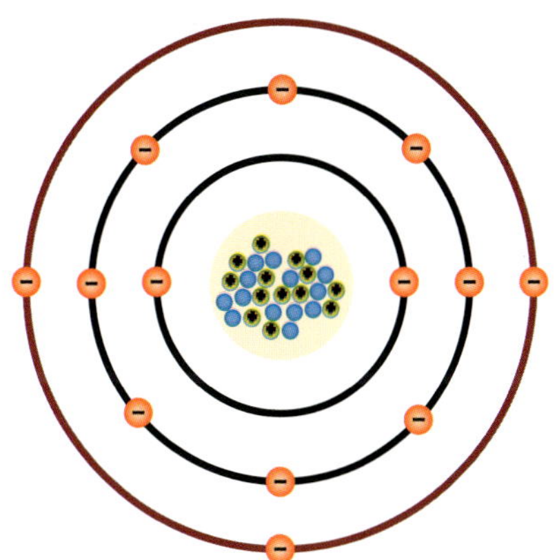

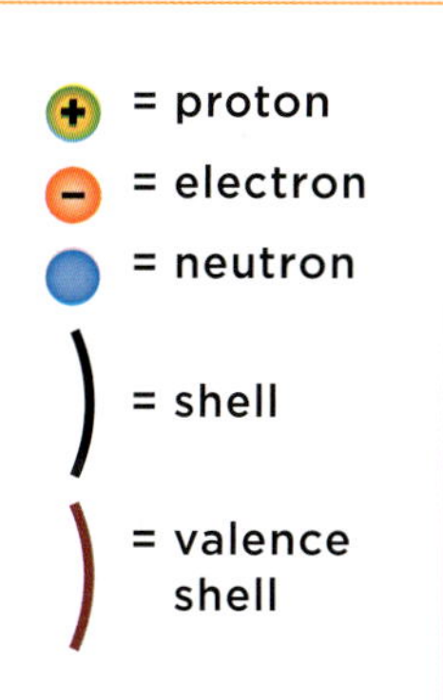

Chapter 5

COVALENT BONDS

The atoms in a molecule are joined together by chemical bonds. These form when valence electrons in one atom react to valence electrons in another atom. Atoms often bond to fill their valence shells. Usually, this means having eight electrons in the valence shell. When an atom has a full valence shell, it is considered stable.

Covalent bonds usually form between two nonmetals. In a covalent bond, atoms share electrons to fill their valence shells. Carbon dioxide is a molecule formed by covalent bonds. This colorless gas is found in Earth's atmosphere.

Sodas are carbonated drinks. They are called carbonated because they have carbon dioxide in them. This is what makes them fizzy! 

Carbon dioxide forms when one carbon atom bonds with two oxygen atoms. A carbon atom has six electrons. Two electrons fill its first shell. The remaining four electrons are in the valence shell. So, the carbon atom needs four more valence electrons to fill its valence shell and become stable.

Oxygen has eight electrons, two in its first shell and six in its valence shell. Oxygen needs two more valence electrons to become stable. The carbon atom shares two electrons with each oxygen atom. The oxygen atoms each share two electrons with the carbon atom. This makes a stable carbon dioxide molecule.

CARBON DIOXIDE COVALENT BONDS

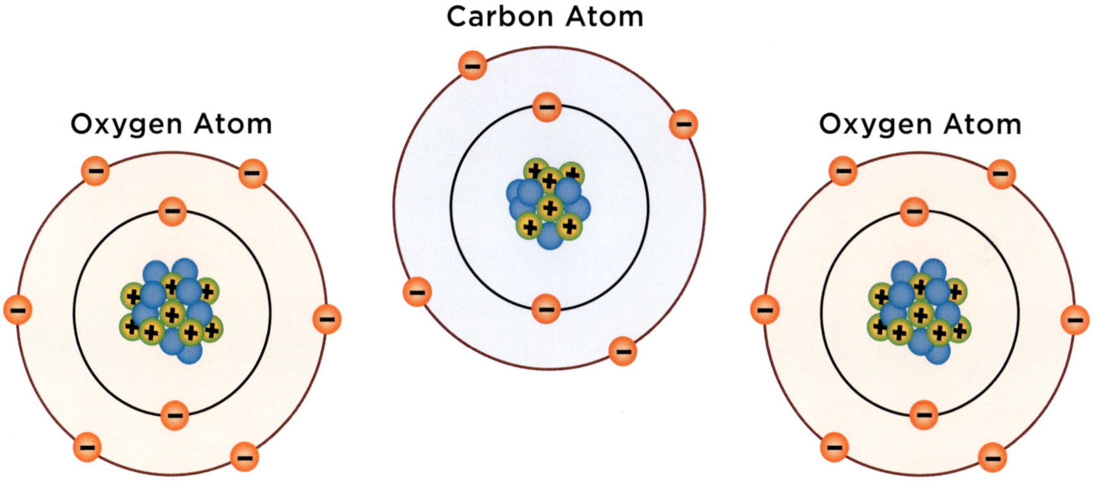

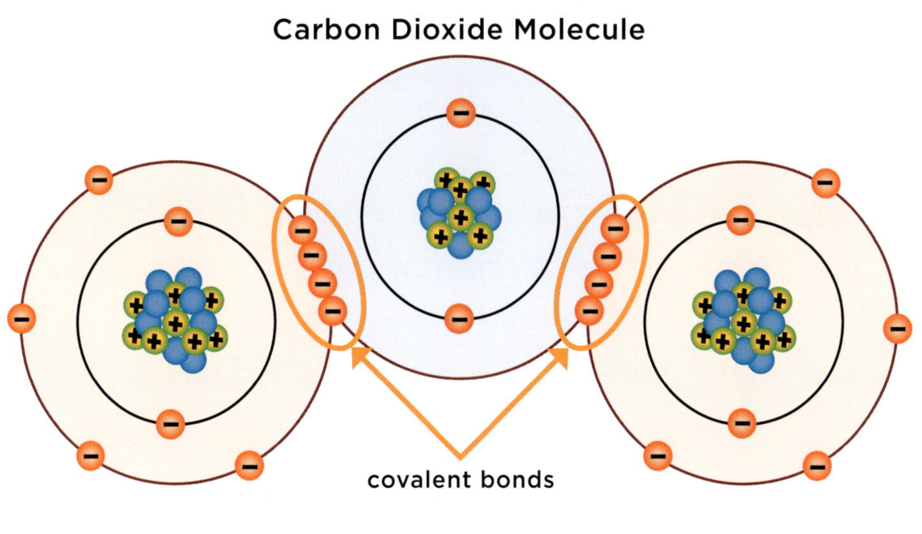

= proton  = electron 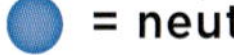 = neutron = shell = valence shell

Chapter 6

IONIC BONDS

Atoms also form ionic bonds. Ionic bonds usually happen between a metal and a nonmetal. In an ionic bond, one atom first gives an electron to another atom. The atoms are then held together by electrical attraction.

Protons have a positive electrical charge. Electrons have a negative electrical charge. Usually, atoms have the same number of protons as electrons. So, the charges cancel each other out and the atom has no electrical charge.

When an atom loses an electron, the atom becomes positively charged. The atom that gains the electron becomes negatively charged. Atoms that have an electrical charge are called ions. A positive ion is a **cation**. A negative ion is an **anion**.

Most toothpaste contains fluoride to help stop cavities. Fluoride is formed by an ionic bond between the metal sodium and the non-metal fluorine.

The chemical name for salt is **sodium chloride**. This is because it is made of sodium and **chlorine** atoms. The atoms are joined by ionic bonds. Sodium has one valence electron. Chlorine has seven valence electrons. Sodium gives its valence electron to chlorine to fill chlorine's valence shell.

Because sodium lost an electron, it becomes a positive sodium ion. Chlorine becomes a negative ion called chloride. Opposite electrical charges attract. So, the positive sodium ion is attracted to the negative chlorine ion. This attraction is what forms the ionic bond.

SODIUM CHLORIDE IONIC BOND

Sodium (Na) Atom
Sodium has no electric charge. It gives its valence electron to chlorine. Since it lost an electron, it becomes positively charged.

Chlorine (Cl) Atom
When chlorine receives an electron, it becomes negatively charged.

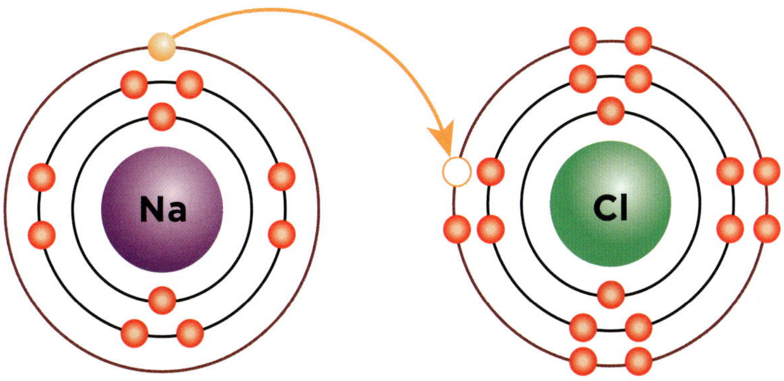

Sodium Chloride (NaCl)
The sodium and chlorine atoms now have opposite charges, so they are attracted to each other. They form an ionic bond.

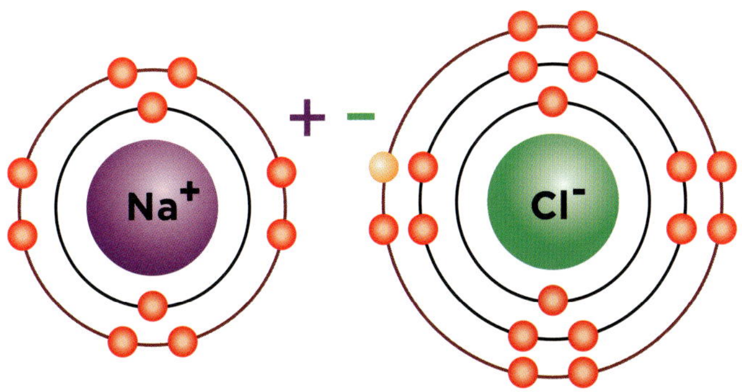

Chapter 7

ISOMERS & POLYMERS

Bonds can affect how substances behave. Some molecules are isomers. These are two substances made of the same atoms. But the bonds between the atoms are arranged in different ways. So, the molecules are different substances even though they are chemically the same.

Glucose and fructose are isomers. They are both sugars made of six carbon atoms, twelve **hydrogen** atoms, and six oxygen atoms. Glucose is the main type of sugar found in our blood. It gives us most of our energy. Fructose is the kind of sugar naturally found in most fruits. Our bodies use it in slightly different ways than glucose.

Some molecules contain just a few atoms. Other molecules, called macromolecules, contain thousands of atoms! Most macromolecules are made of polymers.

Scents are made of atoms and molecules. The rose scent is rose oxide. Rose oxide has four isomers with different scents.

A polymer is a long chain of connected molecules. The proteins and fats in our bodies are macromolecules. Plastic and rubber are macromolecules as well.

MOLECULE MOTION

WHAT HAPPENS

Molecules are always in motion. Heat causes molecules to move faster. So, the molecules in the hot water are moving faster than those in the cold water. The food coloring shows this motion. It spreads quickly in the hot water and slowly in the cold water.

hot water

cold water

MATERIALS

- 2 clear glasses
- water
- food coloring

STEPS

1 Fill one glass with hot water.

2 Fill the second glass with cold water.

3 Place the glasses next to each other.

4 Put a drop of food coloring in each glass.

5 Watch how the food coloring moves in the water. Do you see any differences between the glasses?

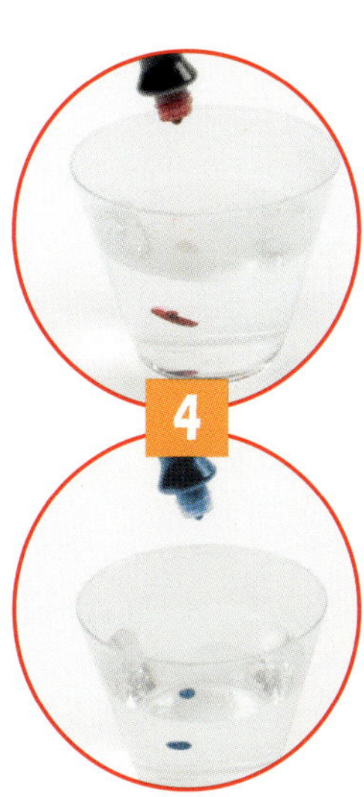

4

EXPERIMENT!

Try the project with a different liquid. Or use one temperature of water. Do different colors of food coloring move faster in the water?

THE SCIENTIFIC METHOD

Want to experiment like a real chemist? Follow the scientific method! The scientific method is a process scientists use to answer questions.

1. Ask a question. Research your question to learn more about it.
2. Develop a **hypothesis**. This is your best guess about the answer to your question.
3. Experiment to test your hypothesis. Record what happens during the experiment.
4. Review the results of your experiment to draw a conclusion. Was your hypothesis supported? Why or why not? Share your results with others.

POLYMER SLIME

WHAT HAPPENS

Glue is made of polymers. Because glue is liquid, its molecules slide past each other. Adding the borax mixture causes the polymers in glue to stick together. This makes slime, which is more solid and rubbery than glue.

MATERIALS

- borax
- water
- measuring cups & spoons
- 2 bowls
- spoon
- white school glue

STEPS

1 Pour 1 teaspoon of borax and ½ cup of water into a bowl. Stir them together.

2 In the other bowl, mix ½ cup of glue with ½ cup of warm water.

3 Add the borax mixture to the glue mixture a little bit at a time. Stir until the glue mixture begins to thicken.

4 Knead the glue mixture until it forms a ball that holds together.

5 You have made slime! What does it feel like? What happens when you pull or squeeze it? Wash your hands after handling the slime.

EXPERIMENT!

What happens if you make the slime with more borax? What about less water? Or, what about a different brand of glue?

GLOSSARY

aluminum—a silver-colored, lightweight metal. It is used in making machinery and other products.

anion (AN-eye-uhn)—a negatively charged ion.

cation (KAT-eye-uhn)—a positively charged ion.

chloride (KLOR-ide)—a chemical compound of chlorine with another element or group.

chlorine (KLOR-een)—a chemical element that under normal conditions is a greenish-yellow gas and has a strong smell.

formula—an expression that uses symbols to say what elements a substance is made of.

helium—a light, colorless gas that does not burn.

hydrogen—the lightest chemical element. It is a gas with no smell or color and catches fire easily.

hypothesis (hye-PAH-thi-sis)—an unproven idea or theory based on known facts that leads to further study.

neutron—a small particle that has no electrical charge. It is part of the nucleus of all atoms except hydrogen atoms.

property—a special quality or feature of something.

proton—a very small particle that has a positive charge. It is part of the nucleus of an atom.

sodium—a soft, waxy, silver-white chemical element. It is found in compounds such as salt and baking soda.

ONLINE RESOURCES

To learn more about atoms and molecules, please visit **abdobooklinks.com** or scan this QR code. These links are routinely monitored and updated to provide the most current information available.

INDEX